HOW TO EARN BUCKS BY SITTING ON YOUR CHAIR IN FRONT OF PC

2

Contents

Online money generating

Web based procuring, otherwise called bringing in cash on the web, and alludes to the most common way of producing pay through different exercises and valuable open doors on the web. It has become progressively well-known and available in the present computerized age. Here are a few key ways individuals can bring in cash on the web:

What Is Content Permitting?

Content permitting is a legitimate plan that licenses one party to utilize one more party's substance under indicated agreements. This content can envelop a large number of media, including text, pictures, recordings, music, programming, and that's just the beginning. The party that claims the substance, known as the licensor, awards the licensee the option to utilize their substance, ordinarily in return for pay, while framing the boundaries in a permitting understanding.

Key Components of Content Permitting:

Content Depiction: The substance should be plainly portrayed, determining the sort, title, and any applicable metadata. This guarantees that the two players see exactly the thing is being authorized.

Permit Extension: This characterizes the degree of the freedoms allowed. It very well may be elite, giving sole freedoms to the licensee, or non-select, permitting various gatherings to simultaneously utilize the substance.

Duration: The authorizing understanding ought to determine the time span for which the substance can be utilized. It very well may be a solitary use, a characterized period (e.g., one year), or unending.

Regional Privileges: This part frames where the substance can be utilized. It very well may be for nearby, worldwide, or worldwide conveyance.

Compensation: Content proprietors decide how they'll be made up for the utilization of their substance. This can include one-time charges, repeating sovereignties, or other installment structures.

Use Limitations: Permitting arrangements frequently remember limits for how the substance can be utilized. These limitations might include altering, reallocation, or sublicensing.

Copyright and Possession: The understanding ought to indicate the copyright status of the substance and affirm that the licensor has the legitimate right to permit it.

End Statement: these frameworks the circumstances under which the permitting arrangement can be ended, safeguarding the two players in the event of debates or breaks.
3. Sorts of Content Authorizing Arrangements:

a. Selective Permit: Awards elite privileges to the licensee, meaning no other party can utilize the substance during the permitting time frame.

b. Non-elite Permit: Permits various licensees to utilize the substance simultaneously, frequently with the substance maker permitting it to a few gatherings.

. Ceaseless Permit: Gives the licensee the freedoms to the substance endlessly, as long as they consent to the settled upon terms.

d. Once Use Permit: Grants the licensee to involve the substance for a solitary case or a particular task or mission.

e. Sovereignty Free Permit: Permits the licensee to utilize the substance without repeating sovereignty installments. They normally pay a one-time expense for the substance's utilization.

4. Security of Content through Permitting Arrangements:
Content makers can safeguard their work through permitting arrangements by laying out clear

and thorough agreements. By indicating use restrictions, checking consistence, and enrolling their copyright with applicable specialists, makers can fortify their lawful position.

5. Ventures Using Content Permitting:
Content permitting is utilized across different businesses, including distributing, media and amusement, promoting, stock photography, programming, and innovation. It assumes a urgent part in these areas by empowering the legitimate utilization of imaginative resources.

In synopsis, content permitting is a basic part of the imaginative and distributing enterprises. Understanding its subtleties and complexities is fundamental for content makers and distributers, as it permits them to share their work while keeping up with command over its utilization, safeguarding their privileges, and producing income from their manifestations.

SELF-PUBLISHING

3. Sorts of Content Authorizing Arrangements:

a. Selective Permit: Awards elite privileges to the licensee, meaning no other party can utilize the substance during the permitting time frame.

b. Non-elite Permit: Permits various licensees to utilize the substance simultaneously, frequently with the substance maker permitting it to a few gatherings.

c. Ceaseless Permit: Gives the licensee the freedoms to the substance endlessly, as long as they consent to the settled upon terms.

d. Once Use Permit: Grants the licensee to involve the substance for a solitary case or a particular task or mission.

e. Sovereignty Free Permit: Permits the licensee to utilize the substance without repeating sovereignty installments. They normally pay a one-time expense for the substance's utilization.

4. Security of Content through Permitting Arrangements:
Content makers can safeguard their work through permitting arrangements by laying out clear and thorough agreements. By indicating use restrictions, checking consistence, and enrolling their copyright with applicable specialists, makers can fortify their lawful position.

5. Ventures Using Content Permitting:

Content permitting is utilized across different businesses, including distributing, media and amusement, promoting, stock photography, programming, and innovation. It assumes a urgent part in these areas by empowering the legitimate utilization of imaginative resources.

In synopsis, content permitting is a basic part of the imaginative and distributing enterprises. Understanding its subtleties and complexities is fundamental for content makers and distributers, as it permits them to share their work while keeping up with command over its utilization, safeguarding their privileges, and producing income from their manifestations.

7. Print-On-Demand: Print-on-request (Unit) administrations are a distinct advantage in independently publishing. They permit writers to print books as they are requested, taking out the requirement for forthright print runs and capacity costs. This guarantees a more practical methodology.

8. E-Books: digital books are a well-known design in independently publishing because of their comfort and openness. Writers can arrange their compositions for tablets or use change administrations given by independently publishing stages.

9. Creator Marking: Building a creator brand is significant for long haul achievement. Writers ought to

think about their composing specialty, ideal interest group, and make a predictable writer persona across their works.

10. Distribution: Independently published books can be conveyed universally through web-based retailers and actual book shops if print-on-request benefits are used. A few writers likewise decide to investigate book recording designs for extra openness.

Independently publishing, with its inventive control and potential for productivity, offers a thrilling road for both nearby and global authors and distributers. Be that as it may, it's crucial for approach it with impressive skill, devotion, and a reasonable comprehension of the market. Eventually, independently publishing gives a chance to creators to impart their accounts and skill to the world based on their conditions.

CONTENT SYNDICATION

Content partnership is a significant procedure in the realm of computerized distributing, and a strategy can help you, as an essayist and distributer, contact a more extensive crowd. It includes republishing your substance on outsider sites or stages to expand your substance's scope and commitment. Here is a manual for assist you with exploring the universe of content partnership.

1. Figure out Your Objectives:
Before you begin partnering content, characterizing your objectives is essential. Is it safe to say that you are going for the gold deceivability, more site traffic, or essentially to lay out expert in your

specialty? Realizing your objectives will direct your system.

2. Top notch Content:
The substance you organization ought to be of the greatest quality. Fundamental it's well-informed, elegantly composed, and locking in. Low quality substance won't yield the ideal outcomes.

3. Select Appropriate Stages:
Recognize stages and sites that are pertinent to your specialty and interest group. These ought to have a decent standing and a nice measure of traffic. Famous choices incorporate Medium, LinkedIn, and industry-explicit websites.

4. Reuse, Don't Copy:
While partnering content, try not to copy it altogether. All things being

equal, reuse it by making slight varieties, like utilizing an alternate title, presentation, or adding new bits of knowledge. This can assist with forestalling Website optimization issues connected with copy content.

5. Legitimate Attribution:
Continuously guarantee that you keep up with appropriate attribution to the first source. This jelly your privileges as well as fabricates entrust with peruses and web crawlers.

6. Partnership Arrangements:
Assuming you're working with bigger distributions, they might have partnership rules and arrangements. Really get to know these terms and follow any necessities they have.

7. Website design enhancement Contemplations:
Remember that partnered content may not add to your site's Website design enhancement as much as unique substance. Be that as it may, it can in any case create traffic and lay out your aptitude.

8. Consistency:
Consistently partner your substance. Consistency is vital to building a group of people and keeping peruses locked in.

9. Advance Your Partnered Content:
In the wake of partnering, advance your articles on your own foundation like virtual entertainment, email pamphlets, and your site. Energize conversation and cooperation.

10. Dissect Results:
Use examination devices to follow the presentation of your partnered content. See measurements like traffic, commitment, and transformations. This information can assist you with refining your system after some time.

FREELANCE WRITING

Surely, I can furnish you with an aide on independent composition. As an essayist and distributer, you might find this data valuable for your work. Independent composing can be a compensating profession, permitting you to communicate your inventiveness and get by from your enthusiasm. Here is an itemized guide on beginning with independent composition:

1. Characterize Your Specialty: Figure out what subjects or classes you are generally keen on and educated about. This will assist you with tracking down your specialty and focus on the right clients.

2. Construct a Portfolio: Make an arrangement of your best

composing tests. In the event that you're simply beginning, consider composing test articles or blog entries on points that interest you to exhibit your abilities.

3. Set Up an Internet based Presence: Make an expert site or blog where potential clients can look further into you. This is a fundamental device for self-advancement.

4. Independent Stages: Join outsourcing sites like Upwork, Consultant, or Fiverr. These stages interface journalists with clients looking for different kinds of content.

5. Networking: Go to composing meetings, studios, and join composing networks. Systems

administration can assist you with interfacing with expected clients and different scholars.

6. Pitching and Recommendations: While going after composing positions, make customized pitches and proposition. Feature your mastery and how you can offer some incentive to the client.

7. Research Your Clients: Prior to tolerating a task, research your clients to guarantee they are respectable and will pay for your work.

8. Pricing: Decide your evaluating structure. You can charge per word, each hour, or per project. Research industry norms to set serious rates.

9. Using time productively: Independent composing demands great time usage abilities. Set cutoff times and stick to them to keep an expert standing.

10. Contracts: Continuously have a composed agreement set up with your clients. This ought to frame the extent of work, installment terms, and cutoff times.

11. Revisions: Be ready to make amendments in view of client criticism. Clear correspondence is significant.

12. Ceaseless Learning: Remain refreshed on composing patterns and procedures. The composing business advances, so continue to work on your abilities.

13. Expenses and Funds: Monitor your pay and costs for charge purposes. Consider counseling a monetary consultant for direction.

14. Construct a Brand: Over the long haul, work on building areas of strength for an as an essayist. Consistency in quality and style can assist you with sticking out.

15. Marketing: Advance your administrations through web-based entertainment, contributing to a blog, and other showcasing methodologies to draw in additional clients.

16. Oversee Dismissals: Dismissals are important for the independent composing venture. Gain from them and continue to persevere.

17. Remain Proficient: Keep up with amazing skill in the entirety of your cooperation's with clients, regardless of whether you experience troublesome clients.

Recall that independent composing can be serious, however with devotion and constancy, you can construct an effective vocation. An excursion includes constant learning and adjusting to the changing requests of the business. Best of luck with your independent composing tries, and I trust this guide helps you on your way as an essayist and distributer.

CONTENT MARKETING SERVICE

Content promoting incorporates different administrations that can assist you with accomplishing your objectives. Here are a few critical viewpoints to consider:

Content Creation: This is at the center of content showcasing. Great articles, blog entries, recordings, info graphics, and more can be in every way created to draw in your crowd. The key is to furnish important data that resounds with your peruses.

Website design enhancement Improvement: Guaranteeing that your substance is web crawler enhanced is urgent. This includes watchword research, on-page Website design enhancement, and external link establishment procedures to work on your substance's deceivability on web indexes.

Web-based Entertainment The executives: Successful substance showcasing frequently includes advancing your substance on different web-based entertainment stages. Dealing with your online entertainment presence, making shareable substance, and drawing in with your crowd is important for this help.

Email Promoting: This help includes making and conveying email missions to your supporters. It's an incredible method for supporting leads, fabricate connections, and keep your crowd informed.

Content Appropriation: Getting your substance before the right crowd is fundamental. Using different appropriation channels, similar to visitor posting on applicable sites or utilizing content partnership, can broaden your scope.

Examination and Announcing: To gauge the viability of your substance showcasing endeavors, following and it is pivotal to examine information. It assists you with pursuing informed choices and refines your techniques.

Content Methodology Improvement: Creating a substance procedure custom-made to your business objectives is major. This incorporates characterizing your interest group, making a substance schedule, and arranging the sort of satisfied you'll create.

As an essayist and distributer, you enjoy a novel benefit in the substance promoting world. Your mastery in making connecting with, very much organized, and linguistically sound substance is important. Joining this with the right happy showcasing administrations can assist you with contacting a more extensive crowd and accomplish your objectives, whether it's advancing your own work or helping different organizations in their promoting endeavors.

Keep in mind, the way to effective substance promoting isn't just about creating content yet additionally grasping your crowd's necessities and inclinations, and reliably conveying content that impacts them. This customized approach can essentially influence your substance advertising achievement.

AFFILIATE MARKETING

Member promoting is a dynamic and worthwhile internet based plan of action that has acquired notoriety both globally and locally. As an essayist and distributer, you're probable acquainted with the idea; however we should dig into it in more detail.

At its center, subsidiary showcasing is a presentation based showcasing technique where people or organizations advance items or administrations through offshoot joins on their foundation. These stages can be sites, web journals, online entertainment, or even email pamphlets. At the point when a guest to your foundation taps on an offshoot connection and makes a buy, you procure a commission.

Here is a breakdown of the critical components of member promoting:

Finding Partner Projects: Subsequent to picking a specialty, you'll have to recognize offshoot programs that offer items or administrations connected with your specialty. Many organizations, from Amazon to specific web-based stores, run partner programs.

Content Creation: As an essayist and distributer, your solidarity lies in satisfied creation. You can create articles, blog entries, item audits, recordings, or some other substance that features the offshoot items or administrations. Your substance ought to be educational and supportive to your crowd.

Promotion: Your offshoot connections ought to be decisively positioned inside your substance. It's fundamental to advance items or administrations in a manner that doesn't seem to be excessively sales. All things considered, center around tending to the requirements and issues of your peruses, with the partner item as an answer.

Following an Investigation: Most member programs give following instruments so you can screen the presentation of your connections. This information is pivotal for streamlining your promoting endeavors.

Compliance: It's indispensable with comply to the guidelines and revelation prerequisites of partner promoting, both at the global and nearby levels. Obviously express your member connections in your substance.

Building Trust: Trust is key in member promoting. Your peruses ought to trust your proposals, so it's essential to tell the truth and just advance items or administrations you really put stock in.

Scaling and Expanding: As you gain insight and get results, you can scale your member showcasing endeavors by making more satisfied, venturing into related specialties, or investigating different subsidiary projects.

Persistent Learning: The partner promoting scene is continually advancing, with new procedures and apparatuses arising. As an essayist and distributer, remaining refreshed is urgent for your prosperity.

In outline, offshoot showcasing offers journalists and distributers a fabulous chance to adapt their substance while giving important data to their crowd. By zeroing in on quality substance, building trust, and ceaselessly refining your methodologies, you can take advantage of subsidiary showcasing both locally and globally.

ONLINE COURSE AND E LEARNING

Online courses and e-learning have changed the location of preparing lately. As a writer and distributer, you're presumably especially mindful of the basic impact these modernized learning systems have had on both overall and close by preparing markets. Could we dive further into this topic?

The Climb of Internet Tutoring:

The web has opened up immense entryways for individuals to get to data and capacities from the comfort of their own homes. With the methodology of online courses and e-learning stages, people presently have the flexibility to learn at their own speed, as per their own inclinations. This has democratized guidance as well as isolated geographical hindrances.

Assortment of Courses:

One of the most exciting pieces of e-learning is the huge number of subjects and focuses open. From academic subjects like science and history to realistic capacities like coding, cooking, and, shockingly, exploratory composition (which is particularly relevant to your profile), there's something for everyone. Online courses deal with the varying interests and needs of understudies.

Overall Reach:

As an overall and close by distributer, you've most likely seen the overall reach of online guidance. Students and specialists can pursue courses introduced by schools and experts from around the world. This globalization of guidance opens up extra open doors for content creation, as you can consider dispersing materials that resonate with a greater, overall group.

Adaptable Learning:

E-learning stages much of the time combine flexible learning propels that alter the chance for development. This fashioners content to individual students' necessities and learning styles. It's an outright exhilarating district for writers and distributers, as making content that is flexible and attracting can significantly constrain.

Challenges and Entryways:

While internet preparing appreciates different advantages, it moreover goes with troubles. Scholarly burglary, for instance, is a basic concern. As a writer and distributer, you sort out the meaning of exceptional substance. Consider researching focuses like falsifying recognizable proof gadgets and approaches for staying aware of the reliability of online guidance.

The Inevitable destiny of Guidance:

All things considered, online courses and e-learning are waiting. As a writer and distributer, you can expect a significant part in shaping the destiny of preparing by conveying predominant grade, remarkable substance that further develops the online chance for development. Your work can add to the improvement of data and capacities on an overall scale, due to the consistently creating universe of e-learning.

CROWD FUNDING AND GIFTS

Are two fundamental parts of financing for different imaginative ventures, particularly in the realm of composing and distributing. As an essayist and distributer, you're probably very much aware of the meaning of these financing strategies, both globally and locally.

Crowd funding:

Crowd funding has acquired tremendous prominence over the course of the last ten years, giving a stage to journalists and distributers to fund their undertakings. Stages like Kick starter, Indiegogo, and GoFundMe offer people the chance to introduce their imaginative thoughts and look for monetary help from an expansive crowd. Scholars can utilize these stages to subsidize their book projects, while distributers can investigate crowd funding to back unambiguous distributions or creative thoughts.

The way to fruitful crowd funding lies in creating a convincing story that reverberates with likely benefactors. Your experience as an essayist is a significant resource in such manner. Recount your task, its importance, and why individuals ought to help it. Offer tempting awards to sponsor, like marked duplicates of your book, selective substance, or restricted version stock.

Drawing in with your crowd is critical all through the mission. Ordinary updates, cards to say thanks, and, surprisingly, in the background content can assist with keeping up with the excitement of your allies.

Donations:

Gifts, then again, are many times a more straightforward type of monetary help for scholars and distributers. They can emerge out of different sources, including people who value your work, artistic associations, or awards from establishments.

While looking for gifts, it's fundamental to underscore the worth of your composition or distributing ventures to society, culture, or a particular local area. Feature your accomplishments and how past help has added to your prosperity. Customized, sincere requests can be exceptionally viable.

Consider banding together with nearby libraries, schools, or proficiency associations that may be keen on supporting your composing tries. Building solid associations with these establishments can open up valuable open doors for gifts, particularly in the event that your work lines up with their objectives and targets.

All in all, crowd funding and gifts assume a crucial part in the existence of an essayist and distributer. Utilizing your composing abilities to make powerful accounts and connect with your crowd is vital to outcome in both these subsidizing roads. Whether you're looking for worldwide help through crowd funding or nearby support through gifts, your capacity to recount a convincing story will significantly upgrade your possibilities of monetary progress in the realm of composing and distributing.

CONTENT EXAMINATION:

Unquestionably, I can give you direction and altering administrations for your substance as an essayist and distributer. Content evaluation and altering are significant stages in the composition and distributing process.

Content Examination:

Content Significance: Guarantee that your substance lines up with the expected message and crowd. Is the point clear cut, and does it address the issues of your peruses?

Construction and Stream: Check in the event that your substance has a consistent construction. It ought to begin with areas of strength for a, trailed by efficient central matters, and finish up really.

Clearness and Compactness: Make sure your composing is understood and succinct. Keep away from language or excessively complex sentences that could befuddle peruses.

Language and Accentuation: Right any syntactic and accentuation mistakes. Guarantee that your substance adheres to the guidelines of appropriate English.

Tone and Voice: Guarantee that your substance's tone and voice are proper for the topic and crowd.

Editing:

Proofreading: Cautiously audit your substance for typographical blunders, incorrect spellings, and little linguistic missteps.

Rewriting: In the event that vital, rework areas of your substance to further develop lucidity, soundness, and generally speaking quality.

Fact-Checking: Confirm the precision of any realities or data introduced in your substance.

Consistency: Guarantee steady utilization of style, arranging, and phrasing all through your work.

Citations: Make sure that any sources or references are appropriately referred to assuming your substance incorporates exploration or citations.

Feedback: Think about looking for criticism from others, like beta peruses or individual authors, to acquire alternate points of view on your work.

Recollect that as an essayist and distributer, keeping up with the quality and honesty of your substance is fundamental. Go ahead and share more insights concerning the particular substance you'd like help with, and I can offer more customized direction.

www.ingramcontent.com/pod-product-compliance
Lightning Source LLC
Chambersburg PA
CBHW071121260726
48661CB00006B/2668